# BREAKING THE BOUNDS

In this impassioned and challenging lecture, Gillian Evans addresses the interdisciplinary nature of the study of medieval texts and its inherent problems, drawing important lessons for teaching and research within the modern university.

Through discussion of the practices, philosophy and constitution of the medieval community of authorship, Evans throws into relief the assumptions which surround our current practice of dividing the subject-matter of study into discrete educational 'portions' by discipline and subject. While acknowledging that the task of pursuing the truth through academic study has perhaps been made more manageable by classification, Evans argues that ancient and medieval scholars would not have flourished in a world of single-subject disciplines. Instead, she calls for disciplinary bounds to be broken and for the modern university to lead in the preservation of learning for its own sake and the fostering of a culture of open-ended enquiry.

G. R. EVANS is Professor of Medieval Theology and Intellectual History at the University of Cambridge. Her previous publications include *Anselm and Talking about God* (1978), *The Language and Logic of the Bible*, 2 volumes (1984–5), *Problems of Authority in the Reformation Debates* (1992), *The Church and the Churches* (1994), *Method in Ecumenical Theology* (1996), and *Bernard of Clairvaux* (2000).

T0349858

G. R. EVANS

∾

# BREAKING THE BOUNDS

∾

An Inaugural Lecture given in the
University of Cambridge
16 February 2004

PUBLISHED BY THE PRESS SYNDICATE OF THE UNIVERSITY OF CAMBRIDGE
The Pitt Building, Trumpington Street, Cambridge, United Kingdom

CAMBRIDGE UNIVERSITY PRESS
The Edinburgh Building, Cambridge, CB2 2RU, UK
40 West 20th Street, New York, NY 10011–4211, USA
477 Williamstown Road, Port Melbourne, VIC 3207, Australia
Ruiz de Alarcón 13, 28014 Madrid, Spain
Dock House, The Waterfront, Cape Town 8001, South Africa

http://www.cambridge.org

First published 2004

Printed in the United Kingdom at the University Press, Cambridge

*Typeface* A. Caslon 10.5/15 pt.     *System* LATEX 2ε   [TB]

*A catalogue record for this book is available from the British Library*

ISBN 0 521 60728 0 paperback

# BREAKING THE BOUNDS

An Inaugural Lecture given by
Professor Gillian R. Evans in the University of
Cambridge on 16 February 2004

For many centuries until the 1820s every graduate of the University of Oxford had to agree never to be reconciled with Henry Simeonnis. Those who wish to know why must pursue the matter in the footnote, which will remain tantalisingly invisible to you this evening, but which I will gladly supply to anyone on request.[1] But, for Cambridge, this evening is bound to have something of the character of the removal of that draconian ban. And this Henrietta is glad to be reconciled.

I am aware that I am at both an advantage and a disadvantage in keeping you here for an hour, since this Inaugural Lecture has not been arrived at inconspicuously. The road to it in the archives of the University is deeply rutted with many footprints and the passage of tumbrils. I expect there are quite a few who have come in

---

[1] R.L. Poole, 'Henry Symeonnis', *English Historical Review*, 27 (1912), pp. 515–17.

the spirit of Augustine of Hippo when he went to hear the sermons of St Ambrose at the end of the fourth century, hoping to be able to write him off. (Old Ambrose had a rhetorician's trick or two; he knew a few things Augustine found he wanted to know, and in the end Augustine, to his considerable chagrin, had to wait in a queue to talk to him.)

But you will be reassured (and not surprised) to know that all this is in the best medieval traditions of our two ancient universities, going back before there were professors, properly speaking. After a stipulated period of practice lecturing and disputation came the formal admission to the guild or corporation, with the inception and the inaugural lecture of the Regent Master which involved exactly the putting up of verbal swords and the exchange of controversy for courtesies which enables us now to spend an hour in this room on serious scholarly questions.

The earliest element to appear in the process seems to have been the expectation that there would be some celebratory eating and drinking. (And this is the moment for me warmly to thank the Faculty of Divinity for its hospitality today.) The conceited Gerald of Wales tells a story of his own prowess as a lecturer in the late 1180s, before even Oxford was really a university, let alone Cambridge. He gave a reading of his 'Irish Places' (*Topographia*

*Hibernica*) to all comers.[2] I am afraid that was in the Other Place. He gave three dinners, one on each day of his three-day Oxford reading. The first day's dinner was, piously, for the poor and needy. To the second day's dinner he invited the most senior scholars, the *doctores* of the 'different Faculties' (*diversorum facultatum*) and their favourite and most promising pupils. To the third day's dinner he invited other scholars and the townsfolk. The whole thing was more of a book launch than an inaugural, and there were no Statutes to be complied with yet, but a proper sense of the priorities is evident already.

In Oxford, as in Cambridge, the Masters were (and remain) the only body of people who could decide to admit someone to join them, for 'nobody in the world could wish a colleague on us'[3] remains our sentiment. This meant that a student could pass the required examinations (with admission to the degree or *gradus*), and even be granted a licence to teach, but still not have been admitted as a Master.

The method of 'incepting' in Oxford survives as set out in December 1431, in the form of a 'statute' drafted by

---

[2] Gerald of Wales, *Topographia Hibernica*, ed. J.S. Brewer, Rolls Series, xxi, 8 vols., 5 (1867), pp. 3–204 and *De rebus a se gestis*, 1 (1861), pp. 72–3; *The History of the University of Oxford*, vol. 1, *The Early Oxford Schools*, ed. J.I. Catto (Oxford, 1984), p. 38.

[3] J.I.M. Stewart, *Full Term* (Methuen, 1978), p. 9.

the Proctors with the agreement of senior scholars.[4] The holder of the new licence sent to each Master the information that he intended to hold his *vesperies*, or 'evening before' ceremony. There might not be a large attendance, for the Masters were not obliged to attend, but the University Church could be full for the inception of someone likely to be exciting or controversial, and it seems that the inceptor could choose the subjects for disputation, with the other Masters present putting in their arguments in turn. This was intended to give the new Master the opportunity to show off his talents and perhaps attract students to his future lectures. When the disputation was concluded the presiding Master was expected to make a humorous but laudatory speech about the new Master-to-be.[5] One such surviving speech emphasises how he profited particularly from the teaching on the natural sciences and as a result he was fired with a passion for philosophy and accordingly went to Paris for the purpose – exactly the sort of teasing reference to the rival show which now goes on between Oxford and Cambridge, though then it was

4 *Statuta Antiqua Universitatis Oxoniensis*, ed. Strickland Gibson (Oxford, 1931), pp. 233 ff.
5 G. Little, *The Grey Friars in Oxford, Oxford Historical Society*, 20 (Oxford, 1891). p. 48. Oxford, Bodleian Library, MS Digby 55.

Oxford and Paris.[6] This pleasant task of panegyric falls today to Professor Ian Leslie as the Vice-Chancellor's deputy and I shall not mind a bit if in his concluding remarks he proposes a visit to Paris for me.

The next day the formal inception was held, in the University Church, where staging was erected.[7] First there was a Mass. One of the Masters then admitted the inceptor into the Guild by placing a cap on his head. The new member read out a text and drew from it two questions for disputation, in verse. The ensuing formal argument was a display piece. The next day, the new Regent Master gave his first solemn lecture, his inaugural. The modern Cambridge professorships are an invention of the late fifteenth century. In 1488 the Regents voted to set up salaried professorships (and students did not have to pay fees to hear these new-style lectures). One result was the decay of the old lecturing requirements which were formerly part of the degree course, and the Regents subsequently had an easier time.[8] But the ancient inception, with its assumptions, is the proper context of an inaugural

[6] *History of the University of Oxford*, ed. Catto, p. 411.
[7] Little, *The Grey Friars in Oxford*, p. 49.
[8] D.R. Leader, *A History of the University of Cambridge* (Cambridge, 1988), vol. 1, p. 242.

lecture given by a professor today, though we have our own modern conventions about delaying it, sometimes until it becomes a valedictory lecture.

The graduating and incepting Masters were faced in those days not only with the tuition fees, but also with some considerable expenses for an occasion like this. Certain 'gifts' to the University administrators were also expected. The Franciscan William Woodford, a contemporary of John Wyclif who practised disputation with him, was on his way back to Oxford to incept in theology with the then enormous sum of £40 for the purpose, when he was mugged and lost it all.[9] He says 'I have never found greater charity anywhere than among the friars when one of them has to Incept in theology.'[10] I have received no intimations that a pour-boire or gratuity will be expected by the University in connection with today's event, but no doubt if I am wrong the Old Schools will be in touch.

Give me an hour, then, and I will endeavour to do two things which should not, I believe, be entirely separated in that Statute D duty of a University teaching officer

[9] E.M. Doyle, 'William Woodford, OFM (c.1330–c.1400). His life and works together with a study and edition of his *Responsiones contra Wiclevum et Lollardos*', *Franciscan Studies*, 43 (1983), 17–187, p. 27.

[10] Oxford, Bodleian Library, MS Bodley 703, f. 49ra.

in Cambridge to foster religion, education, learning and research. I want to look at the assumptions which surround our practice of dividing the subject-matter of study into discrete educational 'portions' by discipline or subject. The late Roman grammarians introduced the student to the Latin language as though it were a kit made up of planks and screws with instructions for assembly, dividing it into sounds and syllables, and discussing the way words are put together from these elements. Cambridge successfully resisted political pressure to adopt the 'bite-sized Mars bar' approach of 'modularisation' a few years ago, but it is still finding it difficult to think pedagogically outside the not much bigger boxes of single-subject disciplines.

But, first, I am going to reflect on the implications of such considerations for future study in my own area of work, the Latin texts of the ancient, early Christian and medieval worlds. For this is the inaugural lecture of a new professor who took an interdisciplinary title.

Words put together in the right way become powerful. The world of classical Greece and Rome understood this so well that the educational system set itself to turn out persuasive speakers, who could not only argue a case but argue it irresistibly. The sixteenth-century Renaissance rediscovered some of these skills in a social and political context in which they began to have a natural place once more. Between the late antique world and the Renaissance stretches more than a millennium of Western European writing, by authors who knew much of the classical Latin corpus and respected it. They could no longer enter without an effort of imagination into the kind of world which produced it, but they used it assiduously nevertheless. This created a more or less conscious 'community of authorship' in which medieval writers strove for a curious like-mindedness with their sources, with the authorities on which they relied, and with each other.

That is a phenomenon so familiar to those who work with medieval Latin texts that it may not strike them as sharply as it should how very singular it is. Here are centuries of intellectual endeavour in which the best, and to our modern eyes most original, minds did all they could to sink their distinctiveness in a pool of shared wording and harmonised ideas.

For a medieval author did not begin with a blank page. He wrote with a consciousness that other minds had been at work, authoritative authors, who were offering him words and phrases and images. He did not hesitate to use them. Indeed, he wrote in others' words for preference if he could. In the view of Augustine of Hippo (354–430), himself among the authors most heavily borrowed from, this was not to be discouraged. Even those not able to compose for themselves may be able to deliver a speech written by someone else. If what they take from others is 'eloquently and wisely written' (*eloquenter sapienterque conscriptum*) and those who 'deliver' the words are themselves good-living men, there is nothing wrong with that,[11] he suggests.

There are exceptions, of course – individuals who express some exasperation with the conventions and restriction of having to work as the humble follower of the greater writers of the past. Adelard of Bath in the early twelfth century explains in his book on the same and the different (*De Eodem et Diverso*) that when he reads earlier authors on the sciences and compares them with the moderns he is struck by the richness of the earlier ones and the comparative silence of the latter. He responded by travelling to the parts of the world where he could talk to Greek and Arabic scholars and learn more of science and medicine than could be got in the West.[12]

In a similar spirit of going it alone, one should not be afraid to find oneself in a minority, asserts Roger Bacon in the thirteenth century, though he relies for comfort on a series of authoritative 'companions'. He quotes: 'You are not happy until the mob derides you' (*nondum felix es,*

[11] Augustine, *De doctrina Christiana*, IV.xxix.62.
[12] Adelard of Bath, *De eodem et diverso*, ed. H. Willner (Münster 1903), p. 3.

*si nondum turba te deriserit*).[13] Authorities are not always right: 'It is fitting to add to the authorities and to correct them on many points' (*in quampluribus*).[14] Indeed, the authorities correct themselves and one another, and dispute what other authorities say.[15] We should prefer truth to authority, and put the authorities right when we can see that they are wrong.[16] With heavy irony, he points out that, for a warrant to do that, we may rely on authority. 'For Plato says, "Socrates my master is my friend but truth is a better friend"' (*Amicus est Socrates, magister meus, sed magis est amica veritas*). A similar alleged sentiment of Aristotle is cited.[17]

Like Adelard, Bacon was reluctant to accept that all the best discoveries have been made already. Human understanding progresses and develops, he contends. One age (*una aetas*) is not enough for inquiry into many of the subjects the authorities have written about. People are aware that many things which will arise in time to come are unknown to us, and in future ages it will be wondered at

13 Roger Bacon, *Opus maius*, Pars 1.5, ed. J.H. Bridges (Oxford, 1970), p. 12. See, not Seneca, as Bacon says, but Sedulius Scotus, *Collectaneum miscellaneum*, IV, 70, CCCM, 67, p. 17.
14 Bacon, *Opus maius*, Pars 1.6, p. 13.
15 Ibid., p. 15.
16 Ibid., Pars 1.7, p. 15.
17 Ibid., p. 16.

that we did not know things which will be then be obvious.[18] Bacon, too, bewails the contemporary neglect of important subjects, *multa quae sunt utilissima et omnino necessaria*, such as mathematics and languages.[19] This was not the spirit of a scholar altogether persuaded of the helpfulness of the 'dwarfs and giants' mentality. The clever idea that writers of later ages are like dwarfs sitting upon the shoulders of giants (*nani et gigantes*) is attributed by John of Salisbury to the earlier twelfth-century Bernard of Chartres. (It is not, as sometimes suggested, Isaac Newton's original idea.) Its peculiar neatness is that, with every appearance of proper humility, it allows the later author to think that he may see more and see further than the 'authoritative giants' could (*plura eis et remotiora videre*).[20] But it requires as a 'given' the acceptance that all useful study and writing is done within a community of existing work.

[18] Ibid., Pars 1.6, p. 13.
[19] Ibid., Pars 1.12, p. 24.
[20] 'Dicebat Bernardus Carnotensis nos esse quasi nanos gigantium humeris insidentes, ut possimus plura eis et remotiora videre, non utique proprii visus acumine aut eminentia corporis, sed quia in altum subvehimur et extollimur magnitudine gigantean.' *Metalogicon*, 3.4, ed. J.B. Hall and K.S.B. Keats-Rohan (1991), *Corpus Christianorum Continuatio Medievalis*, 98, p. 116.

I mention these rugged individualists among many who could be cited, some of whom got themselves into serious trouble with the ecclesiastical authorities. (It was refreshing to hear our new Vice-Chancellor approve of the individual in her incoming speech on 1 October.) The medieval authors who broke the pattern tended to pull at the web which formed the community of authorship only to find out how strong it was. You will have noticed that Roger Bacon devotes a great many words to the citation of authorities for his iconoclastic views on the citation of authorities.

There are important modern educational lessons in all this, of the need to be well aware of existing work in one's aspirations to innovation and discovery. This University's courses assume, at almost every point, that the student should not go away with a degree until he or she knows the way around the work already done in the subject or combination of subjects he or she has chosen. The direction in which I want to encourage you to look is this. Where what is studied is interconnected it behoves the honest scholar both to respect its essential nature and to think critically about old habits of dividing for consideration and the revision of old methods. A balance has to be struck in each generation between the tried and tested and the innovative, which is exactly the balance our community of medieval authors found so difficult and so important.

The members of the classical and medieval community of authorship enjoyed themselves, and there is not much doubt that the struggle to find that balance was one of the reasons why. They express high creative satisfactions. Pliny writes to a friend asking whether it is not time to hand over to others the *humiles et sordidas curas*, the low and dingy cares of his daily life, and betake himself to his studies. His 'business' will then be his leisure; his labour his rest; his wakefulness his sleep.[21] Create something which will be yours for ever, Pliny urges: *effinge aliquid et excude, quod sit perpetuo tuum*. When, after a period of miserable struggle and preoccupation, Anselm of Canterbury made his 'discovery' of a new proof for the existence of God in the late eleventh-century monastery of Bec in northern France, he wrote the *Proslogion*. He describes in the Preface his expectation that 'what it gave me joy to find' (*quod me gaudebam invenisse*) would give others pleasure to read about.[22] This was a true 'eureka'

---

[21] 'Hoc sit negotium tuum hoc otium; hic labor haec quies; in his vigilia, in his etiam somnus reponatur.' Pliny, *Letters*, I.iii.105.

[22] *Anselmi Opera omnia*, ed. F.S. Schmitt (Rome/London 1938–68), 6 vols., vol. 1, p. 93.

experience. The best comforts to be found in this life lie in the study of literature, confirms the twelfth-century chronicler Henry of Huntingdon: *cum in omni fere litterarum studio dulce laboris lenimen.*[23] 'Desire to know letters in such a way that the will to learn possesses your mind and sets it on fire' (*Litteras ergo scire desideres ut animum tuum voluntaria discendi affectio possideat et inflammet*), exhorts Gilbert of Tournai.[24] Aeneas Silvius, fifteenth-century author of the commentary on the doings of the Council of Basle (*De Gestis Concilii Basiliensis*), describes how his friends teased him and cried 'get a life', because it seemed he was going to spend all his time in the company of the poets and orators, and never live it at all. More particularly, was he never going to use his talents to earn himself a living? For the empty blandishments and seductive charms of such company put no bread in his mouth.[25] Unabashed, he puts all this to his proposed patron, Pope

---

[23] Henry of Huntingdon, Prologue, *Historia Anglorum*, ed. Diana Greenaway (Oxford, 1996), p. 2, quoting Horace, *Carmina*, 1.32.14, *laborum dulce lenimen.*

[24] Gilberto di Tournai, *De modo addiscendi*, 1, 2, ed. E. Bonifacio (Turin, 1953), p. 61.

[25] 'Statui saepius ab iis me poëtarum et oratorum lenociniis sequestrare et aliquod sequi exercitium, unde aliquid tandem figerem, quo esset mihi tuta senectus a tegete et baculo.' Juvenal, *Satires*, IX, 139.

Felix V (Anti-pope 1439–49), in the preface to his book on the Council, in the hope that this piece of writing at least will be a breadwinner.[26] He was successful in being taken on as Felix's secretary and in due course himself became Pope Pius II, which in no way undermined his underlying premiss that literary activities are enjoyable.

Somewhere at the heart of all this is the recognition that writing *is* a profound enjoyment, shared by all these diverse individuals who lived centuries apart and knew one another only through the words each generation had left behind for others to read. Remember Boccaccio: 'Poetry is a burning desire to find things out and to write and talk of what you find.'[27] I shall be coming back to that.

What of us, now, as we study these texts? Are we within this community of authorship or outside it, members or observers?

'Quotation . . . is as inevitable as reading, and sometimes identical with it; what else am I doing in reading

---

[26] *De gestis Concilii Basiliensis*, ed. Denys Hay and W.K. Smith (Oxford, 1967), p. 2.

[27] 'Poesis . . . est fervor quidam exquisite inveniendi atque dicendi seu scribendi quod inveneris.' *Boccaccio in Defence of Poetry, Genealogiae Deorum Gentilium*, Book xiv.7, ed. Jeremiah Reedy, Toronto Medieval Latin Texts, 8 (Toronto, 1978), p. 34.

aloud?' asks Patrick Parrinder. An article had appeared in the summer 1999 issue of *Textual Practice* 'shorn of its quotations from the poems of Ted Hughes and Seamus Heaney. Permission to quote them had been refused'.[28] Parrinder went on to explore the implications of a publisher, or an author's estate, refusing to allow normal scholarly use of the materials of study. The medieval community of authorship – which remains ours – stands at the opposite end of the spectrum. Everyone was using the materials, not always with acknowledgement, but with a habit of quotation and allusion so pervasive that in some authors the texture of the writing is that of a close embroidery and hardly a thread of the canvas of the 'author's' own words shows through. Somewhere at the centre of this phenomenon are some very interesting questions about the relationship between 'doing' writing and 'studying' the writing of other people, which stand at the heart of the endlessly problematic situation in which the modern scholar finds himself when he removes the blinkers of the single-subject approach and tries to come at this fresh.

The professor who presumes to give an inaugural lecture in Cambridge need only point to the Statutes

---

[28] Patrick Parrinder, 'Quote, unquote', *Textual Practice*, 14 (2000), 137–44, pp. 137–8.

and Ordinances for authority to do so. But she may have to stand postulant before the community of medieval authors and allow the scissors to be taken to her crowning glory of modern critical skills before she can join them. The medieval scholar with an urge to join the community of authorship faced another complex set of considerations, all bound up with this presumption that it *was* a community and he had to justify the attempt to become a member. The thirteenth-century Franciscan Bonaventure explains that there are four ways of creating a book (*Quadriplex est modus faciendi libros*). Mere scribes copy out the words of others, adding and changing nothing.[29] Compilers also write the words of others, adding to them, but not their own words.[30] Some write both their own words and those of others, but in such a way that others' words form the most important part, and their own words are added merely by way of explanation. Such a one is a commentator.[31] Some, however, write using their own words and those of others, but in such a way that their

[29] 'Aliquis enim scribit aliena, nihil addendo vel mutando; et iste mere dicitur scriptor.'

[30] 'Aliquis scribit aliena, addendo, sed non de suo; et iste compilator dicitur.'

[31] 'Aliquis scribit et aliena et sua, sed aliena tamquam principalia, et sua tamquam annexa ad evidentiam; et iste dicitur commentator, non auctor.'

own words predominate and those of others are included merely for clarification. At last we have the author.[32]

This neat little framework encapsulates the problem which had to be addressed by anyone who wanted to write a book within the medieval community of authorship. No rewards for productivity here; no Research Assessment Exercise or Time Allocation Survey. But there had to be a pretence of a reason. This is paradoxical, given the plentiful evidence that they just enjoyed it, as surely all real writers do. Medieval authors did not like it to be thought that they had just taken it into their heads to write a book. Or, if they had, they were usually careful to put some other construction upon their reasons for writing, in a preliminary apologia. Who am I, the medieval author ought to ask, to add to or try to replace what others have already said?

---

[32] 'Aliquis scribit et sua et aliena, sed sua tamquam principalia, aliena tamquam annexa ad confirmationem; et talis debet dici auctor.' Bonaventure sets out this range of possibilities for the purpose of explaining Peter Lombard's role in composing the *Sentences*. This is the way Peter Lombard has given his opinions, using the views of the Fathers in support ('Talis fuit magister, quid sententias suas ponit et Patrum sententiis confirmat'). His argument is that Peter Lombard ought truly to be called the 'author', even of the book largely made up of quotations from other people's work. Bonaventure, *In Sententiis Petri Lombardi, Proemium,* Q.IV, resp.

There was much (only half-humorous) play with authorial vanity in the ancient world. Pliny teases: 'I think all your writings are fine, especially those which are about me.'[33] 'Your letter pleased me the more because it was long, especially since it was all about my books.'[34] He is grateful to his correspondent for saying he likes his latest writing best, although he himself now prefers the speech he has only just delivered.[35] Medieval authors were expected to disguise their pride in their work, to maintain a pretence. In the medieval community of authorship they were bound to regard themselves as small fry, and to work up quite an *apologia* if they risked writing a kind of book not routinely approved for use within the conventions of the community.

After, 'by the grace of God', Gilbert of Tournai had said goodbye to his responsibilities as Master and Lecturer in Theology at Paris, and brought the shipwreck of his soul to harbour, and set aside philosophy and the babblings of the poets – the stuff of his teaching career[36] – he had, he says, been prompted to write a book. His modesty

33 Pliny, *Letters*, IX.viii.1.
34 Ibid., IX.xx.1.
35 Ibid., VIII.iii.1.
36 'Contuli meas interioris hominis sabbatismum quasi naufragus ad portum, reiiectis philosophorum ineptiis et naeniis poetarum quibus maxime in talibus est utendum.' Gilberto di

topos contrasts the surging waves of the rivers of flowing and overflowing waters (*undas plenissimas influentium et redundantium fluviorum*) those still in the schools have at their disposal in their studies and the despicable fluid so dry and small a person as himself can offer (*tam aridi et pauperculi aquam despicabilem*).[37]

The very notion of plagiarism is foreign to this philosophy of authorship, an invention of a later age. Classical Greek and Latin have no words for 'plagiarism', though late Latin provided *plagium*, for kidnapping. One might well identify one's source, but chiefly to give weight to the borrowed words. There were as yet no footnotes by means of which such borrowings could conveniently be acknowledged. The community of 'authorities', in deference to which, and within which, medieval authors worked, was there to be drawn on, formally or informally. Humbler members of it they might be, but it was their own community of authorship too.

The modern critic − or the modern reader such as the historian, 'using' medieval texts for other purposes − cannot read with a full awareness of the layering process, the endless internal referencing, which is going on. But

Tournai, *De modo addiscendi*, ed. E. Bonifacio (Turin, 1953), p. 60.
37 Ibid.

the attempt has to be made, or the reading of medieval texts resembles a mere sampling of the pie-crust. The steak-and-kidney and the four-and-twenty blackbirds may alike remain undiscovered under the pastry. We cannot ask the medieval author whether we have got him (or occasionally her) right. But we can seek actively to enter his world and speak his language of thought.

Medieval scholarship now embraces a range of specialisms, each of whose exponents has distinct skills and different requirements in approaching a medieval text. As the late Viven Law put it,

from the last third of the nineteenth century on, scholars from a great range of backgrounds – classicists, Medieval Latinists, historians of education and culture, palaeographers, specialists in the medieval European vernaculars, librarians and cataloguers – . . . concerned themselves with grammars and other works on language from the early Middle Ages. Naturally their interests were not those of the historian of linguistics. They asked different questions and found different kinds of activity satisfying.[38]

This tendency to fragmentation and 'specialisation' of approach, even in the relatively small corner of the world of medieval texts concerned with grammar, has

[38] Vivien Law, *Grammar and Grammarians in the Early Middle Ages* (Longman, 1997), p. 4.

its counterparts in every other area of medieval studies. The result has been the appropriation of texts for purposes which might have surprised their authors, because they are our purposes, not theirs. For example, Thomas Aquinas finds himself extracted and the resulting patchwork turned into a 'set book' on 'political thought'.[39]

Medievalists in both teaching and research should be taking a view of the acceptability of using texts in ways which go beyond the original reasons for their writing, and make of them matter for uses which are ours not those of the authors. Complex methodological questions have arisen from critical 'schools' of structuralism and post-structuralism, which have their own vocabulary, even jargon, comprising terms of art which may be fashionable for a brief period only. I will offer you an irresistible example:

It so happens that Pascal occupies the astute man's discursive position, and practices [sic] his discourse of discernment by putting on stage a character who, in the circumstances of fiction in which he finds himself, necessarily discovers what the people and the gentry dissimulate in their ordinary discourses while letting a truth surface in the formula of the maxim that they utter.

---

[39] Thomas Aquinas, *Selected Political Writings* (Oxford, 1948, repr. 1987), ed. and trans. A.P. D'Entreves, for long a set book in the Cambridge History and Classical Triposes.

I do not know what that means. Do you? It is an irony that it occurs in an essay entitled 'On the interpretation of ordinary language'.[40] But such experiments in analysis cannot be written off. We have to take them seriously and decide what to do with them.

The reference of such critical terminology is not at all clear on its face; expressions such as 'structuralist hermeutics', for example, require a gloss. Making sense of terms such as 'intertextuality' necessitates an awareness of the history of critical fashions. It adds a dimension to our task which can also be a distraction. The modern reader of medieval texts has to try to enter imaginatively into the community in which they were written and also to frame a criticism for contemporary use. My own bit of special pleading here is that it should be intelligible and unaffected.

Among the last letters of the aged John Henry Newman occurs a touching series of passages. He wrote to Anne Mozley, who was, at his wish, collecting his letters to make an edition: 'It is very difficult to write you a logically consecutive letter because I have anxious business of various kinds on my mind and my fingers are not what

---

[40] Louis Marin, 'On the interpretation of ordinary language', *Textual Strategies: Perspectives in Post-structuralist Criticism*, ed. Josué V. Harari (Cornell, 1979), p. 241.

they were . . . I wish my hand was so strong and manageable that I could write a letter with a more natural flow of words.'[41] Newman was distressed to find in old age not only that he could no longer form his letters easily but that he began to have problems with expression (and also with spelling, he says).[42] 'It is to me a phenomenon of old age that I cannot write without making mistakes'.[43] Yet, like so many aggressively keen-minded elderly academics, he remained more than capable of taking a view of the literary considerations which should govern the making of the collection of his work. 'I considered that letters, being independent of one another and fragmentary, admit of footnotes without injury to them, but a logical, continuous Memoir does not'.[44] So the author who allows or encourages someone else to collect or edit his writings, even when he is no longer really capable of doing it himself, may retain a strong interfering sense of ownership. The modern editor or critic of a medieval

[41] John Henry Newman, Letter of February 19, 1885, to Anne Mozley, *Letters and Diaries*, 31 (1997), p. 30.
[42] John Henry Newman, Letter of March 4, 1885, to John William Ogle, *Letters and Diaries*, 31 (1997), p. 40.
[43] John Henry Newman, Letter of January 26, 1885, to Lord Blachford, *Letters and Diaries*, 31 (1997), p. 19.
[44] John Henry Newman, Letter of February, 1885, to Anne Mozley, *Letters and Diaries*, 31 (1997), p. 37.

work is able to get on without the indignant comments of the 'author' he is working on, but there remains a question whether there is a duty to consider what he or she might wish; and whether, having considered it, the editor is free to dismiss the author's wishes.

That remains the medievalist's interesting dilemma, whether he is editing a medieval text, or discussing its content and purpose and general contribution to things. This is the leading idea I want to leave with you from this part of the lecture, which is concerned with the texts whose interdisciplinary study I am here to advocate. It behoves the modern reader to do his best to seat himself as securely as he can within the community of authorship as he reads the medieval text. Trying to climb inside the medieval authorial process necessitates some clambering about first inspecting the guttering, the paintwork, the tiles on the roof. But it is also a simple joining in and listening to the preoccupations of the writers we can still read. 'I loved letters from boyhood', claims one Carolingian author (*Amor litterarum ab ipso fere initio pueritiae mihi est innatus*).[45] An affection and a loyalty bound that 'community' in which he recognised himself to be reading and writing. That community remains, to

---

[45] Servatus Lupus, Letter to Einhard, *Epistulae*, 1, ed. Peter K. Marshall (Teubner, Leipzig, 1984), p. 2.

some degree, our own, and respecting it for what it is, is still, I suggest, at the heart of the critical task.

Let me turn now, more briefly, to my promised second main theme. Before the last Research Assessment Exercise,[46] the Higher Education Funding Council for England warned that interdisciplinary work was likely to be undervalued by RAE panels, and this was acknowledged to be partly because they did not know how to handle or assess it. Privately, the organisation which did the underlying research admitted that each conventional discipline had its patch, its territory, and that the interests of those who rose to the kind of respect which got them nominated to sit on such panels tended to reflect that tendency.

The University of Cambridge is not set up at present to encourage students or staff to burst the bounds of single-subject disciplines, or break new ground by creating new disciplines, and that surely cannot be academically desirable. In a speech made in the Senate in May 1974, A.W.F. Edwards remarked that 'those of us who work in the interstices of science are intellectual nuisances, and the price we pay for performing this vital academic function is to be regarded willynilly as

[46] *The HEFCE Report (Ref. RAE 1/99) Interdisciplinary Research and the Research Assessment Exercise*, April 1999.

administrative nuisances. One may sit on five-and-twenty committees and be considered a useful cross-fertilizer, a man of wide experience; but try five faculties, and one is lost.'[47] He was, as he usually is, quite right. Our Statute D.xiv.7, for example, says that 'The University shall assign each Professorship to a Faculty or Department, as appropriate, and may change the assignment from time to time.' The duties of office for all University Teaching Officers include 'devoting' oneself 'to the advancement of knowledge in [one's] subject' (Statute D.ii.4). Statute C makes the Faculty Board responsible for 'prescribing' the subjects in which instruction is to be given in the teaching programme of the Faculty (C.iv.9(b)) and for reporting to the General Board if any officer on the Faculty's establishment is 'not performing satisfactorily the duties of his or her office or is not fulfilling the conditions attached to it'. The Councils of the Schools, clusters of single-subject Departments and Faculties, are increasingly going to be able to direct the University's 'research policy'.[48] And the Resource Allocation Model may strengthen the arms of those who wish to beef up single-subject study, for they hold most of the constitutional cards.

[47] *Cambridge University Reporter* (1973–4), p. 1039.
[48] Annual Report of the General Board, 2002, p. 22.

This is not a speech in the Senate, but an inaugural lecture, so I will leave the situation in the University of Cambridge with those few comments, and turn to the general. The word 'interdisciplinary' has become a flagship term for the launch of research projects and new MPhils, but it is not at all easy to say what it means, taken at large, beyond the confines of the expanse of more than a thousand years of medieval Latin and vernacular texts and their parents and relations. The word seems to have been coined only in the mid-twentieth century: 1937 is the date of the first example in the *Oxford English Dictionary*. The Social Science Research Council was founded to 'deal only with such problems as involve two or more disciplines'.[49] The term was slow in gaining currency and even slower in gaining respectability. Between 1964, when only three societies claimed interdisciplinary interests in the American Council of Learned Societies, and 1985, when all twenty-eight constitutent societies did so, it made its breakthrough. Many long-serving academics of my generation remember the shift from the idea that interdisciplinary work was somehow lacking in essential qualities

[49] For a history of the word, see R. Frank, '"Interdisciplinary": the first half century', in *Words*, ed. E.G. Stanley and T.F. Hoad (Brewer, 1988). See, too, Social Science Research Council, *Report for the Year 1925*, Charles Merriam, Chairman, *American Political Science Review*, 20 (1926), p. 186.

of rigour to the understanding that some subject-matter requires an interdisciplinary approach if it is to be properly understood at all, or if any progress is to be made with it.

Watch the Higher Education Funding Council struggle:

Interdisciplinary research (includes multidisciplinary and cross-disciplinary research). Projects that draw together people and knowledge from discrete fields, each providing a distinctive contribution to the overall field or project. The aim is to bring together diverse perspectives, skills and methodologies from different fields, and subjects. Researchers work in intellectual space between and across fields, and may forge new research fields. Individuals may carry out interdisciplinary research as lone researchers.[50]

I suspect there is a logical fault-line in this between those parts of it which speak in terms of manoeuvres with the original single-subject fields and the notion of 'intellectual space', that free air in which one may occasionally glimpse things quite new.

As to the idea of trying to get a better definition of 'interdisciplinary' by looking at the nature of the subject-matter, here again we come up against the limitations of beginning from what the *Oxford English Dictionary*

[50] *The HEFCE Report (Ref. RAE 1/99) Interdisciplinary Research and the Research Assessment Exercise*, April 1999, p. 4.

calls 'branches of learning' and somehow bolting them together. A trawl through the other leading dictionaries of the moment produces nothing very much better or different: 'subjects of study', 'academic disciplines' are seen as separate things which may come face to face in some way in 'interdisciplinary' work.

This is partly the fault of Aristotle. His contention in the first sentences of the *Posterior Analytics* is that each true 'subject' – such as mathematics or rhetoric – has its own built-in ground rules, some of them self-evident, the others derived from these self-evident truths, but forming a corpus of distinctive principles in accordance with which that kind of knowledge must be explored. The best (and possibly the only genuine) example of this is Euclidean geometry. In the Middle Ages scholars were keen to present subjects which were unfitted for any such treatment as though they possessed 'first principles' in this way. Gilbert of Poitiers, for example, made a list in the middle of the twelfth century.[51] He got on quite well with the first principles of logic and ethics and music and geometry, but he acknowledged himself defeated by grammar, for he had to admit that the detailed grammatical rules of each language are

[51] Gilbert of Poitiers, *Commentaries on Boethius*, ed. N.M. Häring (Toronto, 1966), p. 189.

*positiva*, 'imposed' for that language, and not universal laws at all.

If we look at the subject benchmark statements prepared by committees of academics for the Quality Assurance Agency, we can see that it is no easier in the twenty-first century to square off the ground rules of single-subject study. Thus, 'History provides a distinctive education by providing a sense of the past, an awareness of the development of differing values, systems and societies.' The theologians, by contrast, do not take a position on 'distinctiveness' at all. They see their students 'exploring in an interdisciplinary way the interface between religion and theology on the one hand and literature, culture and the arts on the other'. They favour both 'well-tried methodologies' and ensuring that 'any definition of the subject does not constrain future innovation', whether in response to global trends and issues or new intellectual climates.[52]

A browse through the 'communications' to the Fourteenth International Conference on Patristic Studies last summer might seem to confirm Charles Clarke's worst suspicions that some areas of intellectual endeavour are merely the frogging on the serviceable duffel coat of pragmatic research leading to the manufacture of saleable

[52] Full texts available at www.qaa.ac.uk.

goods. 'Two platonic images in the rhetoric of John Chrysostom'; 'A lost prince in a sermon of Nestorius'; 'An archaic Syriac prayer over oil in an eighth-century chronicle'; 'Irenaeus on gardens'; 'Ritual kissing and early Christian purity concerns'. Then there were the Workshops, a whole series of sessions on such matters as 'Embodied perfection in Dionysius the Areopagite and his first scholiasts'. It has become one of the conventions of the University Orator's annual Oxford offering to entertain those who pack the Sheldonian Theatre at Encaenia with such examples of the erudition and obscurity of the lectures given in Oxford during the year. Yet the moment we really examine these titles it becomes plain that the narrow focus requires the broader grasp. One would need to know something about Plato and classical rhetoric as well as Chrysostom to appreciate the issues raised by the first example; to have an appreciation of the history of liturgy and ascetic ideals in antiquity to make sense of the piece on ritual kissing; for the Workshops you would need to go equipped with a good deal of knowledge – of ideas of embodiment and perfection and the puzzles over the identity of Dionysius and what is a scholiast.

The suggestion with which I want to leave you is that there *is* a general problem, and that it can be articulated something like this. Academic study involves the pursuit of truth with objectivity and rigour. Most academic study is study of 'stuff', subject-matter, evidence, texts, the natural world, even God (or the prior question whether it is possible to study God at all by treating him as 'stuff', a question with which the theologians here will be well acquainted). Historically this has been made manageable by classifying the 'stuff' and devising strategies for saying things about the different kinds of stuff which will stand up to testing and questioning. But if we declassify the stuff and look at it afresh and in different ways, we lose the benefit of much of this work on strategy and present ourselves with jesting-Pilate-sized questions about the very nature of the truth we are seeking. No wonder those RAE panels retreat to familiar territory.

The ancient and medieval members of that community of authorship, which lasted two millennia at least, could not have done what they did in a world of single-subject disciplines. Their work constantly overflowed the attempts to confine it under the subjects of trivium or quadrivium or higher degree study in the three approved subjects of theology, law and medicine. So how can we medievalists achieve more than the odd insight if we wall ourselves in as they did not?

In 1932 there was a discussion in the University of Cambridge about the medical courses. One speaker, Dr A.V. Hill, commented that 'the most fruitful fields were often those on the boundaries of two or more sciences'. He held no brief for physics and chemistry, he said, 'and he was always ready to denounce his physical and chemical friends when he found them, often unconsciously, assuming that those subjects alone represented real science. In spite, however, of their bad manners, he valued their friendship so much that he was most unwilling . . . to cut them adrift.' At this distance of time we do not know whether he said it with a smile, but about one thing he was certainly serious: 'it was necessary either to reform Chemistry in Cambridge, or for . . . people needing education to contract out of it . . . [For] it would be a disaster if Cambridge were wilfully to throw away . . . the fact that by the breadth of its training it tended to produce educated scientific men.'[53] A medieval commentator on Genesis not infrequently took advantage of the opportunity afforded by that passage about the separation of light from darkness at the beginning of the days of creation to accommodate a treatise on optics. Was he an interdisciplinary scholar? Was he breaking the boundaries of the two cultures long before C.P. Snow thought of setting them? Or just following his interests and picking up on those of others?

[53] *Cambridge University Reporter* (1932), p. 303.

Among the criteria provided to referees who are asked to write in support of applicants for Junior Research Fellowships is sometimes to be found 'the candidate's general width of learning'. So that has evidently not fallen out of Cambridge's package of expectations altogether. However, I suspect that few would dispute the heavy preponderance of expectations of excellence in a small area as a safe mark of the outstanding young researcher with high potential. The question is whether a breadth sufficient to enable the scholar to see things with some expertise from more than one angle of view is or ought to be incompatible with doing what is expected within a conventional discipline, and doing it rather well.

Two thousand years ago, Pliny deplored how small the audiences were for poetry readings and the way people tended to slip out before the end.[54] Yet Pliny's experience did not signal the end of poetry or poetry-readings. Much closer to our own time, within that 'medieval' period whose study the Secretary of State for Education dismissed in the spring of 2003 as a mere adornment of academe, the medieval Boccaccio was defending poetry with passion, in the words I have already quoted: 'Poetry is a burning desire to find things out and to write and talk

[54] Pliny, *Letters*, i.xiii.

of what you find.'[55] 'It has sublime effects; for example, it urges on the mind to the longing to speak, to think of unheard-of and rare discoveries.' But he qualifies the enthusiasm with rigour. It also imposes a discipline on the writing which is to communicate all this, for it must be orderly and the right words must be chosen and one must not lose sight of the truth.[56] Nor should the poet go too far with his devices and games with words. He has a duty to be clear.[57] That is not a bad definition of the scholarly calling in general, and it recalls us to the deep questions of what we are here for – which the Government requires us to grapple with these days if we are to defend our academic way of life.

[55] 'Poesis . . . est fervor quidam exquisite inveniendi atque dicendi seu scribendi quod inveneris . . . Huius enim fervoris sunt sublimes effectus, ut puta mentem in desiderium dicendi compellere, peregrinas et inauditas invenciones excogitare, meditatas ordine certo componere, ornare compositum inusitato quodam verborum atque sentenciarum contextu, velamento fabuloso atque decenti veritatem contegere.' *Boccacio in Defence of Poetry*, Book XIV.7, ed. Reedy, p. 34.

[56] Ibid.

[57] 'Obscura aiunt cavillatores his esse persepe poemata, et hoc poetarum vicio, id agencium ut quod inextricabile est, artificiosius videatur esse compositum, idque egisse volunt, inmemores veteris oratorum iussus, quo cavetur planam atque lucidam oracionem esse debere.' Ibid., Book XIV.12, ed. Reedy, p. 50.

But let us not lose sight of Pliny's disappearing audiences. A lecture whose content is not squarely on the syllabus of a particular paper to be taken in the Tripos is at a similar risk of a disappearing audience in our modern University. I have some sympathy with students about this, in the world of tuition fees and loans and needing a good degree to get a well-paid job. I would have less sympathy with a great university which did not take steps to protect studies which are unfashionable for a time, to make space for learning for its own sake and to encourage a culture of open-ended enquiry in its staff and students, without presuming that there will normally be a result which can go into an existing disciplinary box, still less into production in a spin-out company (with apologies to Professor Leslie and the University's endeavours in Corporate Liaison). Not all the most worthy intellectual endeavours of mankind fit in with normative patterns and institutional expectations. Or so those doggedly persistent and boundary-ignoring poets prove.

I shall not resist the temptation to conclude with a sketch of the medieval experience of academic attempts to deal with work which strays outside the appointed boxes. This was a peculiarly complex problem in the Middle Ages, when academic freedom had not been invented, at least not in its modern sense of the belief that the freedom of individual academics to pursue the truth without fear of adverse consequences to themselves is in the public interest. Yet the medieval universities provided the Government with consultants and the medieval equivalents of our 'telly-dons', just as we do today – and they could be just as embarrassing to the politicians of State and Church. A lively example is the fuss over John Wyclif in late fourteenth-century Oxford.

King, Parliament, Pope, University – all had much to play for when it came to the question of who had jurisdiction when a scholar of the University was being accused of heresy. Who had authority to shut him up? And how could it be done? And which authority could tell any of the others what to do?

In late May 1377 Pope Gregory XI issued five Bulls against Wyclif, directed to every power in England which might be able to call him to account. Three were sent to the top men of the Church: Sudbury, the Archbishop of Canterbury, and Courtenay, the Bishop of London. The first of these three bulls contrasted the vigilance in defence of the faith of earlier generations of English prelates with the present negligence in doing anything about Wyclif; it pointed to lamentable similarities between his teaching and that of Marsilius of Padua and John of Jandun. The prelatical pair (or 'at least one of them') were instructed to conduct a secret enquiry into Wyclif's teaching and, if they found that he had indeed been the author of certain doctrines which had been attributed to him, they were to imprison him and extract a confession, sending the offending writings secretly to Rome, while keeping Wyclif under lock and key. Having (presumably) sent this off, the Pope bethought himself of a postscript. He realised that if Wyclif got to hear about this he might hide. He therefore sent instructions that in that event Wyclif should be cited to appear before the Pope within three months, and posters should be put up everywhere he might be, especially in Oxford, to ensure that he knew of the citation. There was a further afterthought, resulting in a third Bull. Scholars were to be found of reliable opinions and sufficient expertise, to explain to the King, his court and councillors that the propositions which were attributed to Wyclif were heretical and a danger to any of the faithful who were brought to share them.

One Bull was sent to the King himself. In it the Pope recognised that no attempt to silence Wyclif could hope to be successful without the support of the King and the secular government. He therefore solicited that support.

The last Bull went to the Chancellor of the University of Oxford. The Pope was displeased that the scholars had allowed false teaching to go on among them. Unless the University suppressed the teaching of a perverse doctrine, and, moreover, seized Wyclif and handed him over to the Archbishop of Canterbury and the Bishop of London, along with any other scholars whose opinions he had infected, the University would lose its privileges.

It all has the ring of a judicious mixture of Charles Clarke and Guantánamo Bay, with the unlikely assistance of our own Rowan Williams. Oxford was not at all sure whether it should be seen to receive this Bull at all, not because it necessarily wished to defend or protect Wyclif, but because it did not wish to acknowledge that the Pope had the right to send the University instructions. Wyclif had his friends there too, and even his enemies might see him as 'one of them' when it came to any challenge from the outside world. Yet it is not difficult to establish that it was jealous Oxford colleagues who had delated Wyclif to Rome in the first place.

Oxford's 'Response' to the letters of the Pope was evasive. The alleged views of Wyclif condemned in the Bull were submitted (*assignatae*) to senior academics for their consideration. Oxford did condemn Wyclif and his supporters, but it did so in an equivocal manner entirely in keeping with the combination of political sophistication and pusillanimity characteristic of the academic mind. It set up a committee (which always conveniently spreads the blame). It put onto the committee a representative selection of safe pairs of hands whose 'expertise' it trusted (*quos peritiores credidimus*).[58]

The decision the scholars judiciously arrived at distinguished between defending the truth of the articles condemned and the concession that they were unacceptably offensive to the ears of the pious. Wyclif indignantly said that what was true should not be suppressed merely to cause offence.

It was argued, after the Regent and non-Regent Masters had consulted in congregation, that it was not appropriate for a subject of the King of England to be put in prison on the orders of the Pope. Nevertheless, Wyclif was invited to consent being confined in the Black Hall in Oxford so as to protect the University from having its privileges taken away: *pro conservatione privilegiorum Universitatis decuit ipsum pati*. In the event his friends got Wyclif released and the Vice-Chancellor imprisoned instead.[59]

In the course of this long-running affair, there was reference to protecting the reputation of the University from

---

[58] *Fasciculi Zizaniorum*, ed. W.W. Shirley, Rolls Series, 4 (London, 1858), p. 113.
[59] *Eulogium historiarum* B, ed. F.S. Haydon, Rolls Series (1863), iii, pp. 347–8.

blame alongside the duty to save the faith from danger and ensure that popular faith is not adversely affected: *et Universitas Oxoniensis non mediocriter diffamata.*[60] So this subtle blending of considerations of truth and considerations of the politics of the real world was already the usual academic way 600 years ago.

Along with other examples of the purposeful pursuit and silencing of medieval academics by embarrassed University authorities, this episode illustrates a group of problems which always faces the scholar who 'questions and tests received wisdom', as the Education Reform Act 1988 s.202 quaintly puts it. There are likely to be cries of indignation that important things are being put at risk (the very souls of the faithful! or the career prospects of graduates); that a committee of reliable senior figures has voted against it; that while the University must on no account brook Government interference, it is anxious not to be disadvantaged in the next funding round (or renewal of privileges) and is therefore sending a copy of its entirely independent decision to comply with the wishes of the Government (or Church) so that its good behaviour may not be put in question. Francis Cornford could have set his *Microcosmographia Academica* in the fifteenth century or the present day with a minimum of rewriting.

[60] *Fasciculi Zizaniorum,* pp. 108–9.

I am not suggesting that a general freeing up of studies to allow those of an interdisciplinary bent freely to follow where the work leads is likely to generate Wyclif-sized huffing and puffing in the Old Schools. But you never know. And we do have to try it.